George E. Atwood

Dictation Exercises to Accompany Atwood's Language

Tablets

George E. Atwood

Dictation Exercises to Accompany Atwood's Language Tablets

ISBN/EAN: 9783337427610

Printed in Europe, USA, Canada, Australia, Japan

Cover: Foto ©Paul-Georg Meister /pixelio.de

More available books at **www.hansebooks.com**

DICTATION EXERCISES

ACCOMPANY ATWOOD'S LANGUAGE TABLETS

FOR TEACHERS' USE ONLY

KERR & POTTER
PUBLISHERS
44 EAST 14TH STREET, NEW YORK

INTRODUCTION.

THERE are two objects to be sought in the work of teaching language. One object is to familiarize the pupil with the forms and idioms of the language and, by daily use of the same, to develop the habit of using them in preference to incorrect forms. The other object is to develop the power to express associate thought in clear and concise English. Although the last-named object is by far the more important one, yet every one recognizes that for the masses of children some drill to teach forms and idioms is necessary. To accomplish this object, a systematic and persistent drill is given in the tablets solely for this purpose. **Occasional** use of correct forms is not sufficient. If the use of them is to become a fixed habit, that habit must be the result of constant use under careful and intelligent guidance.

A large part of all ungrammatical expressions in common use may be grouped under a limited number of topics. Prominent among these are :

The use of **this, that, these,** and **those.**

The use of the verb **be** in its various forms, and especially when the sentence begins with **there.**

The use of **has** and **have** without **got** to denote possession.

The use of the irregular verbs.

The use of **may** instead of **can** in asking and granting permission.

The use of the comparative and superlative forms of adjectives and adverbs.

The use of the defective verb **ought.**

The use of **who** and **whom,** especially in questions.

The agreement of a verb with its subject.

The agreement of a pronoun with its antecedent.

An effort has been made to give sufficient drill on these topics, **throughout the course,** to impress them thoroughly on the mind.

At first glance, the attention will be attracted to the frequency of the lessons in which **is, are, was, were, has,** and **have** are to be supplied. On closer examination, however, it will be seen that in some of these lessons these words are used with nouns, in others with pronouns, and in others when the sentence begins with **there.**

Teachers will notice carefully the method of teaching the correct use of the irregular verbs. It is believed that this plan is entirely new, and yet it is so simple that children easily acquire the power of using them correctly. Teachers know that the use of irregular verbs is a source of numerous errors, both on the part of children and grown people. These errors occur mainly in the use of the past tense and those forms requiring the fourth part, or past participle, of the verb. Constant drill is given on these forms, and it has been proved by use that it is sufficient to develop a fixed habit of using them correctly. Teachers are also asked to examine the methods of teaching the correct use of the forms of adjectives.

To accomplish the more important object in language work, efforts have been made to prepare a systematic course in narrative, reproduction, description, letter-writing, and stories from pictures. Teachers will judge of the merit of this work after a careful examination and use of the same.

The subject of spelling is of necessity closely associated with work in language. The usefulness of knowing how to spell is limited mainly to what one writes. A person's spelling is limited to his spoken vocabulary ; that is, he writes only the words he uses orally. It is, therefore, a waste of time and energy to attempt to teach a child a long list of words; which mean nothing to him, which he does not need, and which he does not and cannot use. Nearly all the spelling that it is necessary or even desirable for children to know should be learned in connection with their work in language. The lessons aim to give the pupil the mastery of a good vocabulary. At the beginning of each lesson are found the new words that may occur in that lesson. There are in all about fourteen hundred words, exclusive of the words that will be needed in the work in narrative, reproduction, description, letter-writing, and stories from pictures.

Simple things in punctuation and capitalization can be mastered by children, but they should be learned from practice. Children should **discover** the rules from the correct use, rather than first learn rules and then try to apply them. In fact, it matters little whether they know any rules, if they know the correct use. Throughout this course of lessons, they have constant practice on the simpler uses of punctuation marks and capital letters.

There is no incorrect work to be corrected, not a rule to be learned, and no technical grammar in the lessons. This thought has been most prominent in their preparation : **"We learn to do by doing, and we form a fixed habit of doing the right by repeatedly doing the right."**

G. E. A.

TARRYTOWN, N. Y., *September*, 1891.

DIRECTIONS FOR THE USE OF THE TABLETS.

Be sure that pupils know every new word before they write.

Have them copy the words at the head of the lesson before doing the other work.

Notice carefully all directions at the head of the lessons in the tablets.

In those lessons where words are to be supplied in blank spaces, pupils are to write the whole sentence each time.

The direction is often given to complete sentences, a part of which is given. In these also they are to write the whole sentence.

They are often directed to copy sentences and make a specified change. Lead them to do this work carefully and make other changes that are necessary.

Often have pupils go over the lesson orally, thus appealing to the two senses of sight and hearing to impress the forms.

In the written work, train pupils to look at the sentence and then write the whole of it without looking at it again. In the original work, train them to think the **whole** sentence before they begin to write it.

Keep a list of misspelled words and occasionally drill the class on them until they know them thoroughly.

Review oral lessons often, and be sure that the children know the reason for using one form in preference to another.

Review the parts of the irregular verbs often.

In all written work, train pupils to think that they must not write a word unless they know it. Write on the board all new words that they may need in the work in narration, reproduction, description, letter-writing, and picture stories.

Neglect none of the work. The teacher may be in-clined to give undue attention to the work of teaching forms to the partial or entire neglect of the more important work. The results in the former work will doubtless be more satisfactory at first, but persistent and intelligent effort in the work of narration, description, reproduction, and letter-writing will surely result in increased language power. The teacher should anticipate the work that is coming in these lines and carefully prepare for it. In this work, always encourage oral language. We need to talk well as much as we need to write well. In fact, our power of language shows itself more in what we speak than in what we write. In writing, we can select our words leisurely and then revise, if we desire. But in speaking, we must have the power of selecting the appropriate word **instantly.**

The teacher may find it desirable to substitute other subjects in the work in narration, or modify the work in other ways ; also to change or simplify some of the work in description and reproduction. Do this, if necessary, but do not omit it.

Where the tablets are used in graded schools, it is recommended that the first and second be used for second year work. In the third year, review the second tablet and use third and fourth. In the fourth year, review fourth and use fifth and sixth.

Directions for the Use of Dictation Exercises.

The dictation exercises are prepared to give additional practice in everything that the pupil does from the tablets. They are made up of sentences, not single words, and no word appears in a dictation exercise that is not given in the corresponding lesson on the tablet or in some preceding lesson. These exercises are not numbered consecutively, because there is not a dictation exercise for every lesson on the tablet. Do not give a dictation exercise, until the pupils have taken the corresponding lesson on the tablet. When there is no dictation exercise to correspond to a lesson on the tablet, give a review exercise.

Teachers should read the work for dictation clearly and distinctly, and **but once.** Pupils must be trained to hear as well as to use their other senses.

FIRST TABLET.

LESSON 1.

This book is new.
Are those boys here?
That slate is mine.
Are those books new?
May I see those books?
These are your pencils.
You may have that book.

LESSON 3.

You and I were here.
Harry and I were at home.
Were those boys here?
Are the slates new?
Are those your pencils?
Were the boys in school?
Those slates are mine.
You may go home.

LESSON 6.

Was your slate broken yesterday, Frank?
The slates were new.
Who broke my long pencil?
He has broken it.
You have broken your slate.
Are those pencils broken?
My slate was broken in school.
May I have a new pencil?

LESSON 7.

Have the mice eaten the cheese?
The child's shoes are poor.
The lamb has soft wool.
Frank has my pencil.
Is this Harry's lamb?
The poor child has no shoes.
You may have those new pencils.
Who ate the cheese?

LESSON 9.

Have the ducks eaten the corn?
Yes, they ate it yesterday.
These pencils are broken.
He has a new pencil for you, Frank.
Were you at home yesterday?
Have you a new slate?
You may have a new pencil.
Write the parts of **break** and **eat.**

LESSON 11.

Have you broken your arm ?
Yes, I broke it yesterday.
The boys ate the oranges.
The mice have eaten the cheese.
Where is Frank's pet lamb ?
The apples were ripe and soft.
Have you an orange for me ?
Write the parts of **break** and **eat**.

LESSON 13.

Were the boys under the trees ?
Those are your flowers in the window.
These pencils are Harry's.
Frank, where are those broken pencils ?
The windows were broken by the bad boy.
Were the birds in the cage ?
Is the boy's slate broken ?
Who ate those large apples ?

LESSON 15.

Have you eaten your dinner under the trees ?
John has broken his new slate.
Who ate your orange, Harry ?
He is eating his dinner.
Have the boys new skates ?
Were all the slates broken ?
You may have an orange for your dinner.
Write the parts of **break** and **eat**.

LESSON 16.

Frank, were the birds in the trees?
How many apples have you given him?
May's bird is out of the cage.
We ate our dinner under the trees.
Where are Fred's skates?
We gave the corn to the chickens.
I have given you seven oranges.
Write the parts of **give**.

LESSON 18.

How many chickens have you, Fred?
He has no slate in his desk.
Have you new skates?
Mrs. Brown has flowers for you.
Have you given it to John?
Yes, I gave it to him yesterday.
Were you at home?
Who gave you the skates?
Who ate all the oranges?

LESSON 19.

Are those Harry's chickens?
The children ate the apples.
Have you a horse, Mr. Brown?
How many books have you?
Ella, is that your sled?
The chickens have eaten the corn.
Who gave you the skates?
Write the parts of **break** and **give**.

LESSON 21.

How many chickens have you, John?
The girls have pretty dolls.
The kitten has a mouse.
Willie and I were at home.
We saw the birds in the tree.
I saw the mice eating the cheese.
Who saw the boy yesterday?
Have you seen my pretty kitten?

LESSON 23.

Who gave the crumbs to the birds?
Harry, how many cylinders have you?
The kitten ate the mouse.
The boy has eaten his dinner.
Those seats are for the girls.
Is this your sister's doll?
Frank's father gave him new skates.
Write the parts of give and see.

LESSON 24.

The girl's dress is blue.
Have you two or three apples?
The mice ate the crumbs of cheese.
Those are Mr. Brown's horses.
Have you eaten four oranges?
We gave two apples to the poor child.
Are the pretty cylinders broken?
Frank's father gave him new skates.

LESSON 26.

Have you seen Mrs. Brown?
Yes, I saw her yesterday.
I saw the pretty bird in the tree.
I gave you those pencils.
The birds ate the crumbs.
Has she given it away?
Yes, she gave it to May.
He has seven pretty chickens.
Write the parts of **break** and **see**.

LESSON 27.

Those roses are very pretty.
May I give sister two?
These three apples are yours.
The spheres are on the table.
May we have our new skates?
I have eaten my dinner.
May I see your chickens?
You may have four oranges.

LESSON 29.

We sat under the trees an hour.
I saw you sitting by the window.
Have you broken the chair?
How many spheres have you?
Frank and I were in the boat.
Were the ducks in the water?
I sat with him yesterday.
Four boys were sitting in one seat.

LESSON 31.

Are you happy, my child?
We saw the bright blue sky.
Who gave the poor boy ten cents?
Is your father sick, Frank?
No, he is very well.
We ate it this morning.
Have you broken your sled?
Have you a rose for your sister?
Has he some water for the horse?
Write the parts of **sit** and **see.**

LESSON 33.

Are you kind to your sister?
The flowers were on the teacher's desk.
The children ate their dinner under the trees.
The boy has four words on his slate.
We saw them before noon.
Is the child's father here?
The bush has no roses on it.
Were both of the girls there?

LESSON 35.

Were you all here yesterday?
No, Frank was at home.
We saw them sitting in their seats.
Have you many oranges to give away?
Yes, we are very happy.
I have broken both pencils.
Who gave you those flowers?
How many spheres have you?
Have you two or three dolls?

LESSON 36.

Who came with you?
Those boys have no shoes on their feet.
How much have you given them?
His father came to-day.
Has the teacher come?
I have two hands and two feet.
You may sit with your sister.
The children have roses for their teacher.
Write the parts of **come.**

LESSON 38.

How was your wagon broken, John?
Each boy has a new book.
How much water have you in the pail?
Have the birds come for crumbs to-day?
Yes, they came this morning.
How many wheels has a wagon?
We saw them coming to school.
Have you given each little girl two roses?
They gave the flowers to the teacher.

LESSON 40.

Willie, who threw the ball?
Have the robins eaten the crumbs?
I have come to see your chickens, Frank.
The bad boy threw stones at the robin's nest.
They threw the kitten into the water.
Have you thrown those apples away?

What have the children for their dinner?
Write the parts of **throw**.

LESSON 42.

This girl's lesson is well written.
We bought shoes for the poor children.
I gave them some crumbs to eat.
My dear child, have you written all your words?
We came to buy some oranges.
Has he written his lesson before?
Has he written a letter to his sister?
Write the parts of **buy** and **write**.

LESSON 45.

Have you written your lesson?
Yes, I wrote it this morning.
We have some crumbs for the robins.
We came to see the boys play ball.
Has he written a letter to his father?
Each little girl has a pretty doll.
Have you some water for the birds?
Were you throwing stones at the robin's nest?
2

SECOND TABLET.

LESSON 1.

Have you written on white paper?
We have bought a basket of nice apples.
Have you a gallon of water in your pail?
Those boys have written their lessons.
How many quarts have you?
I have half a peck of apples in my basket.
Were those baskets full?
I have given the ducks a quart of corn.

LESSON 3.

Pussy's food is meat and milk.
Half of the children are here.
Have you written to your sister to-day?
Have you a gallon of water in your pail?
Who came to school with you this morning?
Have you thrown the pencil away?
Have you given your sister half of the orange?
Write the parts of **throw** and **write**.

LESSON 5.

Harry, who was writing at the table?
Have the chickens grown much?

We have written on white paper.
Have you thrown them away, John?
We were there before you came.
He gave pussy some milk.
Come in, dear child, and eat your dinner.
He grew to be a large boy.

LESSON 7.

Have you been to the store to-day?
The boy's basket has only six quarts in it.
How many quarts of water have you in your pail?
The robin's nest is in that tree.
I have been here many times before.
Are you happy this morning?
The teacher has written the words for you.
We sat there only a short time.
Write the parts of **grow**.

LESSON 9.

Yes, I know he threw the stone.
Our friends came yesterday.
Have you any water in your pail?
No, but I have some milk in it.
They knew it was wrong.
How long have you known him?
How many words have you wrong?
Have you any apples in your basket?
Write the parts of **know**.

LESSON 10.

The children sat on the floor playing games.
We gave the bird some crumbs of bread.
Have the plants any flowers on them ?
Have you a stick a yard long ?
Is it wrong to throw stones at the bird's nest ?
Have you written to your friend ?
How many trees are in the yard ?
Have you given sister any of your orange ?

LESSON 12.

You have too much milk for pussy.
The children were playing quietly in the yard.
Is the lesson too long for you ?
We have been here two hours.
I gave the poor child some bread to eat.
He came to school only one day.
Have you spoken to your father about it ?
We gave the poor boy some bread and milk.
Write the parts of **speak.**

LESSON 14.

How long is the broom handle ?
Frank, have you ever been on that high hill ?
We sat on the grass under the trees.
My brother came home yesterday.
You have given pussy too much milk.
Children, sit quietly in your seats.
You gave the chickens too much corn.
Have you two brothers and three sisters ?

LESSON 16.

Are the ribbons on May's hat new ?
Frank's brother came home yesterday.
We bought three dozen eggs at the store.
Some of your words are well written.
Have you thrown your pencil away ?
Were you glad to come home ?
These pencils are too short.
The bush has eight roses on it.

LESSON 18.

Have you four brothers ?
Yes, and I have two sisters.
Has he eight pencils in the box ?
Have you some fresh eggs, Mr. Brown ?
I have no eggs for you to-day, my boy.
Were you out in the yard under the tree?
Were you there too ?
We have no crumbs for the birds to-day.
Write the abbreviations, Mr., Mrs., Dr., St., Sept., and the abbreviation of the name of your own State.

LESSON 20.

We saw the boy running away.
I never knew that you were his brother.
The boys ran off to play ball.
The rabbits have eaten the apples.
How many rabbits have you, Frank ?
I have never spoken to her about it.
Have you new ribbons on your hat ?

LESSON 22.

Mamma, will you please give me some milk ?
We write on parallel lines.
May's doll has bright blue eyes.
The doors were open half an hour.
Were you very glad to see dear mamma ?
The children have blue ribbons on their hats.
The boy has eight dozen eggs in his basket.
Have I too much bread for the chickens ?

LESSON 24.

Where have the rabbits gone ?
Fred, do you know who did it ?
The bad boy ran away from his home.
The boys did their work well and then ran off to play.
Willie, you have done the same thing many times before.
They have sat under the trees an hour.
Write the parts of **go,** and **do,** and **run.**

LESSON 27.

Mamma, will you please give me some more plums ?
You have come to school late too many times.
Fred's tree has a great many plums on it.
Have you any fish in your basket ?
Has the poor boy a place to sleep ?
He bought six dozen eggs at the store.
Some of the trees have no plums on them.
Have you written a letter to-day ?

LESSON 29.

Have you a cage for each of your birds ?
No, I have only three cages.
He has five plums in his pocket.
They have four boats on the pond.
Have you a sheet of paper ?
Were you in school every day last week ?
May's doll has red cheeks and bright blue eyes.
Have you been in school three weeks ?

LESSON 31.

May, have you eaten your candy ?
No, I gave it to my little sister.
Ella's mamma gave her a pound of candy.
They have written their words on sheets of clean paper.
The rabbit is fond of sweet apples.
We sat under those tall elms an hour and ate our dinner
there.
What have those boys in their baskets ?
How many of the children have ribbons on their hats ?

LESSON 33.

The little boys have warm coats.
Harry and I have always been friends.
Were the best apples given away ?
How many flowers have the girls ?
Each boy has a gallon of water in his pail.
Where are the ribbons for your hat ?
The boy's basket is full of eggs.
The little girl has golden hair and bright blue eyes.

LESSON 35.

Does she like to jump the rope ?
Willie goes to school every morning with his little sister.
Does the boy know where to sit ?
This boy does all his work very well.
Have I too much water for you ?
Has the horse run away and broken the wagon ?
Have you given your brother some candy ?
Write the heading of a letter written from your home.

LESSON 37.

The hawk has strong sharp claws.
The sheep are tame and gentle.
Ida's kitten has a blue ribbon around its neck.
Do you not think that Frank's slate is too small ?
Have you written two letters since noon ?
How many apples have you eaten to-day ?
The hawk's beak is very strong.
Are there black lines on your paper ?

LESSON 39.

Mr. Brown has eight bushels of corn in his wagon.
I have a new pencil seven inches long.
The birds came for crumbs the next morning.
Grace, were you sitting on the ground ?
He sat there alone an hour.
Have you written to him again ?
Write the parts of **go**, **do**, and **run**.

LESSON 41.

Have you sat on the lounge an hour?
Those elms have grown very tall.
Come, Ella, and see this bird's nest.
Does your father know that you are here, Willie?
We can do all our work in an hour.
Have you two brothers?
The children were afraid of the dog.
I said that I was very fond of cherries.

LESSON 43.

Are robins fond of cherries?
Baby has only one tooth.
Rover has strong sharp teeth.
The chickens are afraid of the hawk.
Have you hurt your finger?
Will you please give me some cake?
Have you sat on the lounge an hour?
Have you a knife in your pocket?

LESSON 45.

Are the young robins in the nest?
No, they have flown away.
Could you read your lesson to-day?
We saw the boy, Ida, when he took the teacher's knife.
John says that some one has taken his knife.
Write the parts of **blow, fly,** and **take.**
Write the heading of a letter written from your home.

LESSON 47.

Was the bird's wing broken?
May, do you know where the pictures were bought?
The selfish boys have eaten all the peaches.
Were the apples in the basket or on the ground?
Have you written statements or questions?
Have you a frame for Ella's picture?
Whose papers are those on the desk?

LESSON 49.

Has baby any teeth?
Whose picture have you in your hand?
There it is on the ground.
We have written two questions and one statement.
Come, boys, let us go into the garden and get some cherries.
We saw them sitting on the ground.
Write the abbreviations, Mr., Mrs., Dr., St., Sept., Oct., Nov., Dec., N. Y., and the abbreviation of the name of your own State.

THIRD TABLET.

LESSON 1.

How many blades has your knife?
Does the girl like to play games?
Carrie has eight spools of thread in her basket.
Are the pencils in the box yours or Ida's?
May we boys go home now?
Were all those peaches on the ground?
Write the parts of **run, blow,** and **fly.**

LESSON 3.

Do you want to go into the garden and get some grapes?
John, can you answer my question?
What were you doing, Fred, when I came in?
That is May's sister coming down the walk.
How many of your answers were right?
You were in the class yesterday.
Those pictures have no frames on them.
Have those vines any grapes on them?

LESSON 5.

Willie, have you caught any fish?
Who taught the children to play the games?
Grace, the cat has caught the little robins and eaten them.
I thought they had flown away.
Have you found the teacher's knife?
Does he always try to do right?
Write the parts of **teach, catch,** and **think.**

LESSON 7.

Walter's kite flies high in the air.
I thank you for the bunch of nice grapes.
Ida's answer is wrong.
The knives and forks are on the table.
Grace, have you been in the garden to-day?
Were the large boxes full of grapes?
Are those apples sour?
Whose answer is right?

LESSON 9.

Ella bought two spools of thread for her mamma.
The hawk flies high in the air
Could you write answers to all those questions?
I thank you, Mr. Smith, for these nice grapes.
Have you caught any fish?
Does the rabbit like sour apples?
You said that you were here yesterday.

LESSON 11.

You might have tried it, Carrie.
Have the boys learned to skate?
Boys, always speak the truth.
I know that he tries to do right.
Are the robin's eggs in the nest?
He stood under the tree eating peaches.
Where were you when I called you?
Are those plums sweet or sour?

LESSON 13.

The boys were very rude.
They stood there eating their grapes.
Something must be done about it.
They tried to catch the bird.
John, you are too slow for that work.
Have you nothing to do, my child?
Write the parts of **sit, run,** and **try.**

LESSON 15.

Do not tear the leaves out of your book, Walter.
She wears a shawl around her shoulders.
Were you at church last evening?
They are wearing their new cloaks.
Come, Frank, and take a walk with me in the cool shade.
Write the parts of **wear, tear,** and **walk.**
Write the heading and salutation of a letter written from
your home to your sister who is away from home.

LESSON 18.

Is this your book, Grace, with so many leaves torn out?
The soldiers have no fear.
The boys are on this side of the river.
Do you know where Ida's cloak is?
There the boys are flying their kites.
Does your father know who gave you the picture?
Come in now, boys, and do your work.

LESSON 20.

Do you know whose shawl this is?
He does nothing in school but play.
Pussy sees a mouse in the grass.
Are you always truthful in all that you say?
Are some of the leaves torn out of your book?
We saw you in church last evening.
Have you learned something to-day?

LESSON 22.

Don't you hear the train coming?
He was born Sept. 18, 1880.
Harry, I am sure they were here Sunday.
Yes, I came home Monday.
I'll be there too.
Come, boys, let us try to do just right to-day.
Have you tried it twice?
Yes, and I had the same answer both times.

LESSON 24.

They don't know anything about it.
Will you surely go with me, James?
Who threw the ball through the window?
I wrote the letter Nov. 14, 1885.
The moon is behind the clouds.
I did it myself.
Come, boys, and see Willie's marbles.
He said that he would come Monday.

LESSON 26.

Are you sure he rang the bell?
We came home Monday evening.
We saw a great many pretty flowers.
My child, come in out of the rain.
Kate's work is always well done.
They sat there quietly doing their work.
They didn't do anything wrong.
Write the parts of **fall** and **ring**.
Write the heading and salutation of a letter.

LESSON 28.

Is the surface plane or curved?
Are you sure the bird's wing is broken?
Are those lines parallel?
We saw the boys walking along the shore of the lake.
I don't know anything about it.
The robins have surely flown away.
They just ran through the yard.
Rover, have they given you anything to eat?

LESSON 30.

He was born Dec. 16, 1887.
Yes, I'll write to you Monday.
We saw the children coming along with their teacher.
Were the girls there too?
Have the little birds fallen out of the nest?
No, they have flown away.
Has she any apples in her basket?
I have nothing to do to-day.

LESSON 32.

Mr. Brown, may James go home with me after he does his
work?
They might have known that you were here.
Have the other girls spoken to you about it?
I have seen him only once.
Emma's cloak is almost worn out.
We came to school early this morning.
Have you no rubbers to wear?

LESSON 34.

I am sorry, Lucy, that you can't come to-morrow.
My father says that it is too early for you to go.
Your cousin's new dress is very pretty.
Sister, why have you not written to me before?
Where were you, Henry, when your mother called you?
Are you sure you gave me my knife?
Every day he tries to make others happy as well as himself.

LESSON 36.

We heard the children reading.
Henry, did you hear your father calling you?
Were you in school Tuesday and Wednesday?
I know that Kate's mother wishes her to do right.
Can you make cylinders and cubes out of clay?
We heard the sound of the bell as we came near.
Write the parts of **hear** and **make**.
Write the heading and salutation of a letter written from
your home to a friend.

LESSON 38.

Lucy's new dress is made of green cloth.
Poor child, have you no mittens to wear?
Have you eaten your cousin's orange?
Who came to see me Wednesday?
I ate the grapes you gave me Tuesday.
Does Ida's mamma need her help?
Do you know whose pencils those are, John?
The boy's father came to see the teacher yesterday.

LESSON 40.

Were you there once or twice?
Emma, have you written to your cousin to-day?
Where were you, James, Wednesday evening?
Is Mrs. Smith your aunt?
Have you no other shoes?
Does she come to see you often?
We bought our mittens at your uncle's store.
Write the parts of **wear, tear,** and **try**.

3

LESSON 42.

Which of the two ladies is the taller?
John is the older of the two boys.
This is the shortest pencil in the box.
Is this the longer pencil of the two?
Is James the tallest boy in school?
James has the longest pencil.
He is the oldest man in town.
Have you another orange, Walter?
Those children did their work yesterday afternoon.

LESSON 45.

Grace, were you ill yesterday?
Is Tuesday your birthday?
Harry and I have our share of the candy.
The boys have gone across the river in a boat.
Have you another pair of skates at home?
In which box are the cylinders?
How many ladies were there?
Have you written stories from those pictures?
Write the days of the week.

LESSON 47.

Is Henry lying on the lounge?
They began their work yesterday afternoon.
We asked Emma which book she would have.
Carrie's kitten is lying on the mat by the door.
The boys came home from school before noon, because
they were ill.

Don't you want to lie down, Alice?
I know he was there, because I saw him.
We saw the boys lying on the ground.
Write the parts of lie and begin.
Write the heading and salutation of a letter written from your home to your mother who is away from home.

LESSON 49.

Flour is made of wheat.
Does he like sugar in his tea and coffee?
Is this Willie's birthday?
Were there many boys in school Wednesday?
There are only seven pencils in this box.
I can't write my lesson to-day, because I have no paper.
Fred, are there many plums on your tree?
Has mamma lain down?

LESSON 51.

Papa said he would buy me a new coat, because my old one was worn out.
"The soldiers are coming," said he.
Wouldn't the ladies like to take a ride?
Which of the two boys is the taller?
She was born Jan. 4, 1886.
"How long have you lain here?" asked Walter's mother.
The lady said, "Yes, James is a good boy."
They can't go with us, because their mamma is ill.

FOURTH TABLET.

LESSON 1.

"Where were you yesterday?" asked his teacher.

The children could not go to school, because their shoes were poor.

How many oranges ought I to give sister?

The younger horse is the better one of the two.

The man said, "I have surely broken my arm."

What ought we to do about it?

"You did very wrong, Harry," said his father.

They ought not to have taken it.

LESSON 3.

I can't do that, because I am sure it is wrong.

"Have you another knife at home?" asked Frank.

Frank, you ought not to whip your pony.

They lay down and went to sleep.

The shorter pencil is the better one of the two.

The man said, "I will give you ten cents a quart for your cherries."

The children were beginning their work as we went in.

LESSON 5.

He could not come last week, because his father was away.

How many of our oranges ought we to give away?

" Somebody has taken my hat," said the boy.

They ought not to do those things.

The lady said that the children were asleep.

He can't work to-day, because he broke his arm Wednesday.

" Did you have a pleasant visit ?" asked his mother.

Which of the two boys is the younger ?

Write the heading and salutation of a letter written from your home to your aunt.

LESSON 7.

Grace said she could not go without her mamma.

The hungry children came in for their supper.

I know you were in the room, because I heard your voice.

Have you eaten the whole of your orange ?

" I am sorry my little boy is so saucy," said his papa.

The angry boy struck his little brother.

Fred, have you eaten your breakfast ?

Whose picture have you in your hand ?

LESSON 9.

You ought not to be saucy to your parents.

I know there were seven plums in the basket, because I counted them.

The children said, " We have no father."

Whose knife have you, George ?

They ought not to go there alone.

" Ought I to give sister the whole of my orange ?" asked Alice.

Did you have a pleasant visit at your aunt's ?

Write the abbreviations, Mr., Mrs., Dr., N. Y., Sept., Oct., Nov., Dec., and Feb.

LESSON 11.

Have you enough sugar in your coffee ?
This is the fourth time I have spoken to you about it.
" Be careful, my child," said her mother.
How many can you count in a minute ?
There are eight ladies present.
The shorter pencil is the better one.
You ought never to be saucy to those older than yourself.
" Couldn't you come yesterday ?" asked his teacher.

LESSON 14.

How much money have you, George ?
We came to school together this morning.
Are you sure that is Walter's voice ?
There are eight ounces in half a pound.
We sat on the ground only a few minutes.
" Mamma, I love you very dearly," said little May.
They could not buy bread for the children, because they
had no money.
Were there seven violet cubes in the box ?
He goes to school every pleasant day.

LESSON 16.

Is your father better ?
Yes, he seems quite well to-day.
Which of the sticks is the longer ?
" Were you angry with your sister ?" asked his mother.
She seems to be happy in her work.

Does George know whose knife it is?
The girls might have gone without their brother.
James could not go skating, because his skates were broken.
Were there many grapes in their basket?
Write the heading and salutation of a letter written from your home to your sister.

LESSON 18.

Can you walk a mile in an hour?
"Sometimes you do your work very well," said his teacher.
George, are there many fish in this brook?
John's sister is Frank's aunt.
Which is the seventh day of the week?
There were seven knives in this box.
"Can't you wait a minute?" asked his father.
I am sure this is Henry's brother.
Are there eight shelves full of books?

LESSON 20.

The man's horse ran away and broke the wagon.
She has many friends, because she is always kind and pleasant.
There were only a few girls there.
The man said, "I will see you about it Wednesday."
Are there any ladies present?
Yes, I have looked on every shelf.
Were you at home on your birthday?
"Will you go with me to-morrow?" asked George.
You seem quite ill, Alice.

LESSON 22.

Which is the larger apple of the two?
What ought we to say to them?
Lucy's book is on the sixth shelf.
Hasn't your father come, James?
The boy said, "I can't do that, Mr. Brown, because it is wrong."
You ought not to go without your cloak.
Will you surely go with me to-morrow?
Is this the highest house in town?
I know I ought not to do that.

LESSON 24.

My dear child, were you naughty in school to-day?
How long have you lain on the ground?
How many trees are there in the field?
"Does your mother know it?" asked her cousin.
Can you jump over that high fence?
Is the sparrow's wing broken?
The fox is very cunning.
May I have a piece of your orange?
The sparrows have come for their breakfast.

LESSON 26.

Have the birds flown out of sight?
May's birthday is Wednesday.
Those trees were blown down yesterday.
Did this great oak grow from an acorn?

" I am sure they were there," said George.

Henry, how many buttons have you on your coat?

He was born Aug. 14, 1888.

We could not go to school last week, because we had no shoes to wear.

Write the heading and salutation of a letter written from your home to your cousin.

LESSON 28.

The naughty boy cried, because he could not have his own way.

There is a new sponge for you, Walter.

Have you kept your brother's ball all this time?

She cries for May's doll.

Were there any pears on this tree?

Is that money yours or your father's?

" We all had a jolly time," said she.

There are eight quarts in a peck.

You ought not to have broken it.

LESSON 30.

Have you torn your new apron, Cora?

Each one has his own work to do.

" Which book have you read?" asked his teacher.

None of your friends were there.

How many pears have you eaten to-day?

Whose slate have you, George?

" You might have done better," said his father.

Were you there too?

I have seven pieces of money in my hand.

LESSON 32.

Have you broken the tumbler, Emma ?
" What have you in the pitcher ? " asked her mother.
We began the work last week.
Willie's slate is the wider of the two.
Have you been naughty to-day ?
The boy said that he had broken his arm.
May we look at the pictures in your book ?
Are you sure that you gave her a piece ?
The man said, " I will see you to-morrow."

LESSON 35.

Has each one a piece of toast for his supper ?
What have you on your wrist, Cora ?
" That is very queer," said Walter.
Did you get any apples ?
There were none there.
Do you like the pure cold water ?
How many geese are on the pond ?
They have nothing to do to-day.
" Whose cloak is that ? " asked Lucy.
We walked to school together this morning.

LESSON 37.

My child, you will lose your ball in the tall grass.
We were very busy all day.
How much have you earned to-day, George ?
A boy ought not to spend all the money he earns.

Have you been absent many days?
Does this pleasant weather make you happy?
The thirsty children are glad to get the pure cold water.
" I am too busy to play with you now," said his mother.
Write the heading and salutation of a letter written from your home to a friend.

LESSON 39.

There are more flies than we can count.
He ran all the way up the steep hill.
Is the comb made of rubber?
Are there enough hoes for all the boys?
The man could not hear what we said, because he was deaf.
" Can you jump over the wall?" asked the man.
There were only three pears on that tree.
Do you like the pleasant weather?
Have you been very busy all day?

LESSON 41.

The boy said that somebody had taken his knife.
Which is the sixth day of the week?
The teacher said, " I can't help you now."
Were you at home Wednesday?
My father said that I had done the work well.
The child lay on the ground asleep.
"Were you absent yesterday?" asked the teacher.
The teacher said that you were saucy.
The children came to school together.
" I have no time for that," said he.

LESSON 43.

Have the butterflies flown away?
" I am very tired," said the child.
We ought never to do wrong to please our friends.
There was no carpet on the floor.
Were there curtains at the window?   .
Ought I to give away half of my grapes?
The children tried to catch the butterfly.
Is the smaller orange the better one?
Have you been absent many days?
" I am too busy to read to you now," said his mother.

LESSON 45.

Whom did you see?
Were the oxen in the field?
For whom did you buy that pretty picture?
Do you like this pleasant spring weather?
Whom do you know here?
With whom did you walk yesterday?
Have you given each one a piece of your candy?
The poor children cried for something to eat.
Were you tired after your long walk?

LESSON 48.

Emma, we have brought you some pretty flowers.
The careless boy never does his work well.
Whom did you meet on the way?
With whom did you play this forenoon?
" George, you are too noisy," said his mother.
Have all the blossoms dropped from the tree?

He always seems to be honest.
The children stopped a minute to speak to their teacher.
Are these true stories, Alice?
Have the butterflies flown away?
Write the parts of **drop** and **stop**.
Write the heading and salutation of a letter written from your home to your brother.

LESSON 50.

How many berries have you, Henry?
There were no more blossoms on the tree.
Apples and pears are ripe in the autumn.
Lucy's birthday comes in the summer.
Are there any sheep in that field?
No, I can't go with you to-morrow.
We began the work Aug. 7, 1889.
There is no coffee for the children.
The child's shoes are almost worn out.
Are there any eggs in the sparrow's nest?

LESSON 52.

" How do you do, little boy?" asked the man.
There is not a careless child among them.
Is your birthday in the summer or autumn?
Soon the little girl said, " I am very sorry."
To whom have you written to-day?
The teacher says that you are too noisy.
Whom have you asked to help you?
" I have brought you some berries," said James.
They were absent Monday, Tuesday, and Wednesday.
Write the abbreviations of the months.

FIFTH TABLET.

LESSON 1.

We walked very slowly all the way.
There were horses, sheep, cows, and oxen in the same field.
That is the prettiest flower among them all.
Who threw the ball through the window?
You can easily do your work in an hour.
Which is the thinner piece of paper?
I am sure there were eight knives in the box.
Which rose is the prettier?
Whose knife have you, George?
He does his work neatly every day.

LESSON 3.

Did you have a pleasant time at the picnic?
Whom did you meet there?
They have not been absent a day this week.
To whom did you sell your book?
We sat on the ground in the shade of the maple tree.
March, April, and May are the spring months.
The children were tired when they came home.
With whom does he sit in school?
The teacher said that we were making too much noise.
Whom will you ask to help you?

LESSON 5.

Have you finished your work, Carrie?

" I have the prettier doll," said Grace.

Are you always honest in all that you say?

Were you punished for doing wrong?

He could not finish his work, because he was ill in the afternoon.

The naughty boy scared the butterflies away.

Hasn't she begun her work?

Yes, she began it this afternoon.

This is the longer, stronger, and better one.

Write first, second, third, etc., to ninth.

Write the parts of **finish, punish,** and **scare.**

LESSON 7.

Are you eleven years old, my boy?

We met the merry children coming home.

Were there any bees on the flowers?

The winter months are December, January, and February.

I hope you do not feel cross this pleasant morning.

Mr. Brown sells children's shoes.

Has he anything to eat to-night?

The little boy's leg was broken below the knee.

Whom did you see there?

Are you sure Harry's rabbits are both dead?

LESSON 9.

" Did you have a pleasant time at the picnic?" asked his friend.

We finished our work before noon.

He dropped his basket of eggs and broke three dozen.

The teacher said, "I will give you an hour to finish your work."

She came in, walked across the room, and sat down.

I am afraid you stopped by the way to play.

They scared the butterflies away.

"We were too late for the train," they said.

We walked more slowly coming home.

LESSON 11.

There were pears, peaches, oranges, and grapes in the basket.

He has eaten the greater part of his candy.

We came across the lake in that small boat.

They sat on the ground only a few minutes.

You gave the smaller orange to the larger boy.

I'll go as quickly as I can.

Have you some pretty autumn leaves in your basket?

Is the larger apple the better one?

Can you write rapidly?

Couldn't you go without your father?

The younger boy ran more rapidly than the other.

LESSON 13.

Do you know whose fault it is?

The boy has bread and potatoes for his breakfast.

The man has fourteen barrels of apples in his wagon.

There were a great many people here yesterday.

Whom do you see, Fanny?

Is this your sister's bonnet?

We saw the boy to whom you sold the knife.
We saw a large number of children coming down the walk.
Whom did you hear say that ?
The ladies stopped, asked the boys some questions, and then went on.

LESSON 15.

Are you writing every word neatly ?
I couldn't visit you yesterday, because I was ill.
" Have I slept four hours ?" asked the boy.
Lie down, Carrie, and rest yourself.
We were afraid of losing our ball in the grass.
The robins will not come again, because you have scared them away so many times.
Boys, be honest, kind, and true.
The boy was punished for running away from school.
Emma, is that your new bonnet ?
Have you finished your work, George ?

LESSON 17.

Are you sure there are sixteen ounces in a pound ?
Are the child's parents dead ?
The teacher told us many funny stories.
She rang the bell until all the children came in.
I know there were only seven in the box.
Are the bird's wings both broken ?
He said he would come as quickly as he could.
Isn't this flower the prettier one ?
June, July, and August are the summer months.
Write the days of the week.

LESSON 19.

" I came early this morning," said he.

I think you have the larger piece.

The man said he would buy your berries.

Were all the children at the picnic ?

" Whom have you seen to-day ? " asked his father.

" What have you in your mouth ? " asked his teacher.

He said that there were a great many people there.

Are you eighteen years old ?

Then he said, " Yes, I know it was wrong."

The teacher said that you were absent Wednesday.

The streets were full of men, women, and children.

LESSON 21.

The night was cold, dark, and stormy.

We have seven beautiful roses for you.

About whom were you talking ?

She came forward and sat by the teacher's side.

Was either one of the girls here ?

There were three tiny eggs in the nest.

He was running backward and fell down.

He thought he had broken his arm.

Some people always seem to be happy.

Neither one of them was here last week.

We caught eight beautiful butterflies.

LESSON 24.

In whose book are you writing ?

There the boy stood in the middle of the street.

Is there a key for each door ?

The children came running toward us.

Have you anything for either of them?
Has the farmer milk, butter, and cheese to sell?
The farmer's wife makes butter and cheese.
Whom did you send for it?
Do you know whom I saw there?
Whom did the teacher punish?

LESSON 26.

The boy's father died June 14, 1876.
You rang the bell too early to-day.
Have you lived here eighteen years?
The soldier lay on the ground dying.
Isn't he doing his work too rapidly to do it well?
She was born Jan. 12, 1889.
Somebody has surely taken my pencil.
Yes, we passed them on the street.
What may we do, mamma?
Neither one of them was there.
We have two eyes, two ears, two hands, and two feet.
Write the parts of **live**, **die**, and **cure**.

LESSON 28.

The children came in, sat down, and began their work.
Were there good reasons for your absence?
I have some beautiful pansies for you, mamma.
Are there more than fourteen here?
The poor boy's breakfast was bread and potatoes.
The farmer's son and daughter were with him.
"Here are some pretty daisies," said Kate.
Mamma, didn't I go quickly?
There are both white and yellow daisies in the basket.
Were there three stormy days last week?

LESSON 30.

"What may we do?" asked the boys.
We can't visit you until next week.
The teacher said that we were good children.
September, October, and November are the autumn months.
Neither of us knew whose book it was.
Frank said, "I did the best I could."
Are they still sitting there under the trees?
He said that he was fourteen years old.
They gave good reasons for their absence.
"Run away, dear child," said her mother.

LESSON 32.

We would gladly have done it for you.
The smaller boy is the stronger one.
Which one has the more money?
He always walks very slowly.
Is the taller boy the younger?
Which of the two has the more friends?
Go as quickly as you can, my child.
Which of the two boys is the older?
They ought not to throw stones at the nest.
What ought we to do for them?
The children were poor, dirty, and ragged.

LESSON 34.

The child ran against the tree.
We walked beyond the oak tree and then sat down to rest.
Are those barrels empty?
No, they have potatoes in them.
Has any one spoken to you about it?

We came up the walk, across the street, and into the house together.

There are fourteen apples in the bottom of the basket.

There was nobody there to help me.

Neither one of them was there.

" Go as quickly as you can, my child," said her mother.

LESSON 36.

He can't go to school to-day, because he has no shoes to wear.

Men, women, and children ran through the streets.

Walter, will you lend me your knife?

Are you sure he meant to do it?

Was there a good reason for your absence, Carrie?

I wouldn't do that, because it is wrong.

Is your cousin eighteen years old?

Come, boys, let us climb this maple tree.

Is it too far for us to walk?

I know they were there, because I saw them.

LESSON 38.

I thank you for your kindness to me.

Do you know whether the boy's arm was broken?

Were there four squirrels in one tree?

Is Kate's sister nineteen years old?

" I will gladly help you," said he.

There are eight quarts in a peck.

Does the farmer's son have a happy life?

The bees get honey from the flowers.

There were no oranges for them.

He called the boys to him, gave them each five cents, and told them they might buy some candy.

LESSON 40.

" Have you a letter for me?" asked his mother.

This great man was born Sept. 16, 1868.

My friend said that he had met you before.

Each child has books, paper, and pencils.

The boy's mother died May 8, 1879.

His father said, " You did right, my boy."

I am not sure whether I can go.

Her mother said that she had gone away.

Mr. and Mrs. Brown came home yesterday.

" I thank you for your kindness," said the boy.

Nobody seems to know what to do.

LESSON 42.

I am sure you will often find it useful.

You gave me an apple instead of a pear.

You are in danger there, my child.

The teacher talked to them very kindly.

Is the taller boy the younger ?

We walked more rapidly coming home.

The two boys tell different stories.

Do you know whether there were many absent ?

Those flowers are very pretty indeed.

I gave two oranges to Harry, three to Kate, and four to May.

LESSON 44.

Readers, spellers, slates, and pencils were given to the children.

I think those readers are different.

We did our work on the blackboard.

She sat in the parlor an hour.
Have you learned to play the piano?
I am sure he meant to do right.
Neither one of the boys was there.
Are you nineteen years old to-day?
How many classes are there in school?
Have you spoken to anybody about it?

LESSON 46.

Have you forgotten it all so soon?
We can't go skating to-day, because the lake is not frozen over.
Are the children enjoying themselves?
Yes, they seem to be very happy.
Will you forget the teacher's kindness to you?
They began the fourth reader last year.
She lay on the lounge in the parlor.
The boy spent three cents for candy, two cents for a pencil, and had eight cents left.
Write the parts of **forget** and **freeze**.

LESSON 48.

Are there any wild animals in the woods?
Have you ever seen a camel?
There were squirrels and monkeys in the trees.
Some bears are very fond of honey.
Are birds, fishes, and insects animals?
Would you be afraid to meet a lion?
I have forgotten how many were there.
There are nineteen boys in Henry's class.
Neither one of the boys was in school to-day.
Are all the potatoes in the barrel frozen?

LESSON 50.

Have you forgotten what I told you, Joseph?

" Have you enjoyed your visit, Mabel?" asked her mother.

Does Maud know how to play the piano?

Then he said, " I surely meant to do right."

" There is nobody to help us," said he.

The boy's father died June 16, 1874.

Have you scared the squirrels away?

You might have done it yesterday.

They must have forgotten to ask about it.

These animals have eyes, teeth, tongue, and feet of the same kind.

SIXTH TABLET.

LESSON 1.

She spoke to me pleasantly this morning.
The box is three feet long, eighteen inches wide, and eleven inches deep.
Which is the larger?
Were you in earnest, Minnie?
This is the better one.
How many are spoken of in the last statement?
He is always willing to help his sister.
They would gladly have done it for you.
Is Joseph the older?
He is the tallest man in town.
You could have done your work easily in half an hour.

LESSON 3.

Did you see the rainbow after the shower?
We came home before sunrise.
To whom did you say you gave the knife?
Have the boys new clothes?
Yes, they bought them at Mr. Brown's store.
The poor boys have no blankets to keep them warm.
The shower soon passed over and we went out.
The morning was clear and the afternoon cloudy.
He always seemed very earnest in his work.
The child has new clothes, new shoes, and a new hat.

LESSON 5.

Will you surely remember your promise, Mabel?
Children, do you always obey your parents?
They were silent for some time.
" My dear child, what makes you so unhappy to-day ?"
asked her mother.
I am sorry you have forgotten your promise so soon.
The girls are always willing to help each other.
There are many reasons why you should obey your parents.
The lion, tiger, and bear are wild animals.

LESSON 7.

How many colors are there in the rainbow?
I am sorry you have such a bad habit.
Were all your words correct?
We bought beef and mutton at the market.
We gave the chickens six handfuls of corn.
Have you a good excuse for your absence?
The grocer sells tea, coffee, and sugar.
Is your brother twenty-two years old?
Have you a quire of paper in your box?
She has gone on an errand for her mother.
There were no unhappy children among them.

LESSON 9.

There are twenty-four sheets of paper in a quire.
" How many colors are there in the rainbow?" asked his
father.
Have you broken your promise, my dear child?
He does errands for his mother every day.
" I am sorry my little girl is so unhappy," said her mamma.

The man spoke to me very pleasantly and said, "Good morning, my little man."

She has red cheeks, blue eyes, and golden hair.

Soon the boy said, "I took the money, Mr. Brown."

Do you remember the teacher's kindness to you?

LESSON 11.

There are apple trees, pear trees, and peach trees in the orchard.

Is Joseph the younger?

The chimneys were blown over by the strong wind.

Rover ran on ahead of us and came home first.

Who is the younger?

The girls walked more slowly than the boys.

They enjoyed the whole day very much.

Are there any daisies in the meadow?

Is Minnie the oldest?

The children came into the kitchen for something to eat.

LESSON 13.

Children, whom should you obey?

The girls have gone to the meadow for daisies.

Have you seen the beautiful rainbow?

Whom have you sent?

The boy's clothes were old and worn.

We came into the garden before sunrise.

To whom have you given it?

There was a light shower in the morning.

For what have you spent all your money?

They stopped to speak to the ladies.

The parts of the body are the head, trunk, and limbs.

LESSON 16.

I have not forgotten your great kindness to me.
Have you ridden twenty-two miles to-day?
Each child carried his own lunch to the picnic.
Has one horse drawn the wagon up that steep hill?
Maud, we have saved part of the fruit for you.
The boy went into the house, sat down by the window, and seemed very sorry for what he had done.
Is this the fourteenth of the month?
The father could buy no bread for his children, because he had no money.
The boy's illness has kept him in the house a long time.

LESSON 18.

There are a great many spruce trees in that forest.
The children held a picnic in the grove.
There were eight boys and twelve girls at Mabel's party.
The children seemed to enjoy the sport very much.
Have you a peck of chestnuts?
" I will go as quickly as I can," he said.
Along the banks of the river were willow trees.
Chestnuts are ripe in the autumn.
We have ridden nineteen miles to-day.
There are maple trees, beech trees, elm trees, and chestnut trees in the forest.

LESSON 20.

Are you truthful in what you think, what you say, and what you do?
Joseph, have you hidden the boy's hat?

We had fine sport swinging in the grove.
We enjoyed ourselves every minute.
Neither one of the boys has a home.
I don't know whose slate it is.
The children sang very well indeed.
We found daisies in the meadow.
Boys, be in earnest in everything you do.
There were only three good pears among them.
The boys have gone to the orchard for apples.

LESSON 22.

The birds sang sweetly in the trees.
Are you thankful for all you enjoy?
Is that a proper thing for you to do?
She was very patient through her long sickness.
He is brave, polite, and manly.
Some people are much more generous than others.
The teacher seemed pleased with the pretty flowers.
He is always prompt at school.
Which rose do you think is the prettier?
Couldn't you have gone more quickly than you did?
You could have done the work more easily another way.

LESSON 24.

The picnic gave the children much pleasure.
"Are you Mrs. Brown's niece?" asked the lady
How many pupils are there in your school?
I have seven pieces of silver money.
Whom did you strike with the whip?
We heard the birds singing in the trees over our heads.
By whom have you sent the flowers?

Are you patient when everything seems to go wrong ?
Do you know whom she has sent on the errand ?
Gold, silver, and iron are useful.

LESSON 27.

We sat there an hour listening to the singing of the birds.
The picnic gave the children much pleasure.
Mabel, have you studied your lesson ?
The man stopped his horses, gave each of the boys an apple, and then drove on.
Was the teacher satisfied with your work ?
She had many friends, because she was kind to everybody.
He always seemed willing to help others.
"I am too busy to read to you now," said her mother.
We stopped to look at the beautiful flowers.
The poor children seemed very grateful for the new clothes.

LESSON 29.

Have the turkeys eaten the corn ?
The sick boy could take only a few spoonfuls of milk.
Are the towels and napkins made of linen ?
There were twenty-two children at Minnie's party
Are there no swallows around the barn ?
Have all the pigeons flown away ?
The pupils sat in their seats quietly studying their lessons.
The teacher seemed satisfied with the child's work.
There was nothing wrong in your work to-day.
Chickens, turkeys, and geese were in the yard.

LESSON 31.

The boy's father died Jan. 16, 1886.
Joseph was then fourteen years old.

" I am much pleased with your work," said Mr. Brown.

I don't know whether they came or not.

Great oaks from little acorns grow.

We enjoy the bright sunshine after so many stormy days.

" Do you obey your parents?" asked the man.

She is unkind, selfish, and unhappy.

Have you forgotten your promise?

Do you remember whom you saw there?

LESSON. 32

Can't you play together peaceably?

We ought to be patient and cheerful.

You ought not to be selfish and greedy.

The younger boy is the more generous.

We came home at nine o'clock in the evening.

You may go whenever you are ready.

The children were quiet and peaceable.

Are you satisfied with your new piano?

Sit here, Maud, until I come back.

The teacher came into the room, looked at each slate, and went out again.

LESSON 34.

The boys are always peaceable and happy.

We saw the children hurrying to school.

"You may go whenever you are ready," replied her mother.

We reached home at eight o'clock that evening.

There are two pints in a quart, eight quarts in a peck, and four pecks in a bushel.

Children, couldn't you play together peaceably?

Whom did you call to help you?

She said that she would remember her promise.

Whom will you send to the market ?

The child tried to be cheerful and patient through her long illness.

LESSON 36.

How long have you lain there ?

I laid the book on the table.

I lay down to rest.

Have you lain on the lounge an hour ?

We sat under the trees listening to the singing of the birds.

She set the chair by the window.

He seems to be very unhappy, because he can't have his own way.

Yes, we lay down on the ground.

Some people are never satisfied with anything.

The boy has a knife, a top, two pencils, and twelve marbles in his pocket.

LESSON 38.

Are you in trouble, my child ?

We had a very pleasant ride in the carriage.

In how many different cities have you lived ?

Can Minnie's parrot talk ?

There were several children there at eight o'clock.

The man said that he felt satisfied.

The man stopped, thought a minute, and then went on with his work.

Rover followed us wherever we went.

I laid the book on the table.

It is lying there now.

They lay down on the ground in the shade of the tree.

LESSON 40.

" There are several reasons why you must stay at home,"
replied his father.

The children said they were playing together peaceably
and quietly.

" My dear child, are you in trouble to-day ? " asked his
teacher.

The teacher said that we had lain on the ground long
enough.

You may have a ride in the new carriage to-morrow.

We came home from the picnic at five o'clock.

Will you tell your mamma your secret ?

She was a very lovable child.

The teacher took my slate, looked at my work, and said
that it was well done.

LESSON 41.

I received the letter June 4, 1889.

No one believes that you did wrong.

The teacher said that we must walk more slowly.

We expected several friends to visit us yesterday.

Are you the taller, Minnie ?

Which of the two girls is the older ?

I think this is the prettier picture.

Is he kind, polite, and cheerful ?

The younger boy is the larger and stronger.

" You must obey your teacher," replied his father.

We stepped aside to let the ladies pass.

LESSON 43.

Your disobedience is the cause of all your trouble.

We spent the whole afternoon looking for the lost money.

We write on our slates, on paper, and on the blackboard.

The man said that he was satisfied with my work.

From whom do you expect a letter to-day ?

I was very much pleased to receive an answer to my letter so soon.

My child, have you forgotten your promise ?

The carriage was drawn by four white horses.

How many children are there in the family ?

There are four boys and three girls.

LESSON 45.

We laid the books on the stand.

They are lying there now.

The children set their chairs near their mamma and then sat down to listen to the story.

We looked for the squirrel but could see nothing moving in the trees.

Yes, we stayed there until three o'clock.

The boy was punished for his disobedience.

The girls could not come to school yesterday, because they expected their cousins to visit them.

Thursday, Friday, and Saturday were pleasant days.

LESSON 47.

We met in the morning, at noon, and again in the evening.

Every one of the boys was absent.

The man's strength is very great.

The larger room has the higher ceiling.

Does the teacher believe the boy's story ?

I received my sister's letter yesterday.

Neither of the boys was disobedient.

" I hurried as fast as I could," replied Frank.

Those boys seem to have no disposition to please their teacher.

Is either one of them expected to-day ?

Have you studied all your lessons ?

LESSON 49.

" I am pleased with your willing obedience," said their teacher.

Do you find pleasure in disobedience ?

We saw something moving slowly in the bushes.

The boys said that they did not believe it.

There were several children in the carriage.

" How long may we play in the grove ? " asked the children.

" You must come home at four o'clock," replied their mother.

They hurried home to tell their mamma about the picnic.

The naughty boy said that he did not care for his punishment.

The little girl has a pleasant and cheerful disposition.

The boy is polite, truthful, earnest, and obedient.